Supermarket Sarah

WonderWalls

WonderWalls

A guide to displaying your stuff!

CICO BOOKS

LONDON NEW YORK

Published in 2012 by CICO Books
An imprint of Ryland Peters & Small Ltd
519 Broadway, 5th floor, New York NY 10012
20–21 Jockey's Fields, London WC1R 4BW

www.cicobooks.com

10 9 8 7 6 5 4 3 2 1

Text © Sarah Bagner 2012
Design and photography © CICO Books 2012

A CIP catalog record for this book is available from
the Library of Congress and the British Library.

ISBN 978 1 908170 82 8

Printed in China

Copy editor: Hilary Mandleberg
Designer: No Days Off
Photographer: James Gardiner
(Front cover photo: Alexandra Bootherstone;
page 3 wall created by Fred Butler; walls on
pages 8, 14, 16, and 17 by Sarah Bagner, styled
by Elkie Brown; photo on page 13, bottom, by
Bruno Conrad)

For digital editions visit
www.cicobooks.com/apps.php

Contents

L♥Ve YoUR STUFF!

This book is about embracing everything you own and showing it off on your walls. Whatever your taste, it's about celebrating the unusual, the beautiful, the eccentric, and the simple.

In this book I have visited homes and studios around the world, choosing inspirational designers and collectors who use their walls to display themselves and their treasures. There is a diverse range from the minimalist to the hoarder. The walls range from the macabre to the romantic, from vintage to brand new. Collectors come in all shapes and sizes—some celebrating contrasts, some hoarding private stashes, some squirrel stuff away in boxes, others show stuff off like a peacock. Some walls are very much ever-evolving works in progress touching on details, others are grander and more explosive in their statements. I'm fascinated by both functionalists and the splendid nature of the ornate decorator.

I love to
experiment with
visual ideas on a
wall, moving items
around and finding
their perfect
harmony. Often I
find items which
don't fit together
and in this case
it is their
opposing nature
that I enjoy. For
example, I love
collaging together
odd pieces of
found printed
material. Seeing
things out of
context, playing
and twisting
conventional
notions, fascinates
me. It is seeing
the absurdities
in life and the
humor of it that
is important to
me in my creative
process.

➜➜This is my "Neon" wall, created at home
for SupermarketSarah.com. I wanted it to be a
burst of color and fun, so chose bright neon
yellows, pinks, blues, and greens. I brought
the vintage flamenco dress in a flea market
in Spain and it takes pride of place here.
The vintage Yves Saint Laurent spotty shirt
was sourced by my Aunt Katya (an incredible
vintage scout!) from a Swedish market—I love
it and was sad to see it sold. The trainers,
hung by their laces, are refugees from an
indecisive fashion moment—I couldn't decide
which color to buy so bought two pairs in
different hues. I have sold one "pair" and am
now stuck with odd trainers forever—something
which I hadn't quite bargained for!

Whatever is displayed, and however it is displayed, all the walls
in this book are displayed with heart. There is a certain truth and
honesty about each wall, nothing appears contrived or twee.
The walls are expressions of the owners' personality, not their
status. Everything has a meaning for its owner. From collections
of supermarket receipts, records, and shells, to fine art,
chandeliers, and porcelain—whatever it may be, I love a story.
Items only have the value you put on them and this book explores
the ideas and thoughts behind the displays and why these
objects, when adorning a wall, help us discover ourselves. The
walls are revealing, amusing, and thought-provoking, and I hope
will inspire you to look at your own collections with a fresh eye.

Supermarket SARAH

CLICK ON ITEMS TO BUY

This mixed wall is full of thoughts. The champagne lamp at the bottom left, made by designer Sascha Kipferling, is an idea we had to upcycle vintage lampshades and champagne bottles with a lovely fabric cord. I found the bull horns in Brighton market and I use them for display. Carrying them home on the train was an awkward yet amusing experience! The effort put into bringing flea-market finds home give your purchases an added experience which means you cherish them and have a special connection with them.

Supermarket Sarah.com

⬆I often try to work around one idea or theme, and color is often the most simple and striking concept—this red wall is bright and bold. The "Jesus Loves Me" banner is made by artist and designer Phoebe Eason and is inspired by one that I bought in an African Christian store. I sold the original one on my stall at Portobello market to Damon Albarn from the band Blur, who just happened to be passing by. I was very excited about this as Damon was my childhood idol! In his honor I commissioned Phoebe to design more banners in this vein and they have become a Supermarket special!

➔I created this blue wall for the site and also for *Blonde* magazine's blue issue. The blue flowery swimming cap is my favorite—I have a penchant for granny stuff!

My own journey started in 2009. Eager to do something that was my own, I decided to combine my interests in fashion and vintage with some new ideas on how to sell online. Supermarketsarah.com is based around the idea of a real "wall" on which I display and sell my items. From vintage fashion and customized objects, to a selection of work by up-and-coming designers as well as some unexpected curios, everything is a one-of-a-kind piece with a story about its discovery.

←This is my "Royale with Cheese" wall, set up in Selfridges department store in London for their Concept Store 2010. It incorporates Royal vintage-themed items and the nod to the movie Pulp Fiction highlights that the wall has a modern and fun spin, too. This 30-foot high wall was my first venture into Selfridges and I sold a variety of vintage and new designer pieces. The giant papier mâché elk head sits proudly at the top, with an oversized polystyrene pearl necklace draped over him. Styling this wall was a huge leap from displaying items on my home wall, and the installation was terrifying yet totally exhilarating.

Supermarket Sarah struck a chord with a blogosphere thirsting for invention. On zero budget I went live with my first "wall" from my living room. Before I knew it, I had press and bloggers at my doorstep and I was displaying my wares on a 30-foot high wall in Selfridges department store in London. Since then, I have expanded the site to feature the work of many designers and have been amazed to be working with top designers, who I've known of and loved, as well as a plethora of upcoming ones. The walls have moved into bars, shop windows, galleries, and reception areas.

Supermarket Sarah has become the place to go for inspirational delights and is regularly featured in media across the board, from magazines to the BBC News. The site and blog have evolved into a platform for young designers as well as being at the core for key events and sales that I put on throughout the year.

This "Clash Mash" themed wall was created for Selfridges' London Concept Store 2010. This wall is an anarchic clash of color and pattern. The cardboard rock-style guitars form a cross bow at the top, and the "Soft Rock" scarf by Bethan Wood hangs inbetween. There is a feeling of 80s "anything goes" with this wall. It is a riot of color and fun.

⬇This stretch of wall in the Selfridges' giftware department in 2011 was my Supermarket Sweep of walls—the stark, functional pegboard wall stood out against the traditional look of this luxury department store. Here I sold a variety of vintage and new designer Supermarket Sarah giftware. The pegboard gave me the flexibility to remove and replace items easily. Themes changed topically and evolved according to customers' tastes.

These are my recycled business cards. I source fun, colorful packaging and cut out interesting sections, then stamp the back with my logo. Supermarket Sarah is all about making something from nothing and these cards were the starting point for me. They are very much what my brand stands for.

← I love collecting visuals with a sequential nature and often use type-cases to display little treasures. The framed pictures show collections of 50s cigarette packet designs. The 1950s certificate is from my father— he was an Olympic table tennis champion in his youth. The graphic design is beautiful.

→ My Portobello market stall in 2009 included collections of figurines and objects, as well as vintage clothes and a few new designer pieces. This is where it all started. Being on the front line of a market stall is where I got my experience of buying and selling. I love the no-nonsense approach of market selling. Here anything goes and there are no rules to visual merchandising, you simply have to try it and see what sells—you soon learn! It was always a rather terrifying yet wonderful experience, but I loved the camaraderie of the market vendors and organizers and learning the unwritten rules of market vending etiquette.

At the core of Supermarket Sarah, and one of the main reasons I think it resonated with the zeitgeist of the moment, was its personal approach and that's very much what this book is about. It's about celebrating your own individual style! In a world where styles and trends are often dictated to us, I want readers to embrace the personal. I have always loved market shopping because it's personal and I love the tales behind objects and the questions they provoke. When I had a stall in London's Portobello market, what I enjoyed most was the personal interaction I had with my shoppers and this is what I wanted to re-create virtually on my site.

→When I'm out and about, I always keep an eye open to finding vintage treasures. They are my triggers which spark little thoughts and glimmers of ideas.

↓Bathrooms are the perfect gallery space for the unconventional. On the walls I have displayed Henrik Delehag's weird and wonderful art collection. The silver crown is made by the brilliant props and accessories designer Fred Butler and was lovingly made for a Selfridges Christmas window. It has also been worn by Patrick Wolf for the front cover of *Super Super* magazine.

→→Your living room wall is your first port of call in home display. I actually found this mantelpiece dumped on the street and by chance it fitted the fireplace space perfectly—it seemed like fate! There is an almost religious feeling to creating mantelpiece displays as they are shrines to our ideas and beliefs in creativity.

My own walls are a real mixture. I love trawling flea markets and finding trinkets, mixing them in with family photos and found objects. Breathing new life into old objects and giving them new meaning brings me great pleasure. Discovering a pile of old encyclopedias abandoned in a market was very exciting as they have become perfect display stands. I found the "EGGS" sign left on a cardboard box on the street. The typography is rather beautiful so I use it as a centerpiece.

Painting objects lovely bright colors is always fun. I dragged these balsa wood parrots back from a trip to Amsterdam and painted them up—I like the fact that they have traveled with me and become part of something new. The portraits show men with fantastic moustaches and beards and are the start of a collection.

I treat my walls as my sketchbook. They are full of little thoughts and ideas which may lead to more. We build up a visual memory of things as we grow up, and I like my walls to remind me of all the fun thoughts that make me, me!

Here's to wearing your heart on your walls! Thank you to all the home-owners in this book who showed me their hearts!

Chapter 1

Hoarder's Delight

Maxi Minimalism

Ilse Runow Raihle has had a keen interest in art, design, and fashion since she was a child, when she was often to be found gazing in awe at her grandfather's cabinet of curiosities. She studied anthropology and is today a librarian and journalist.

She loves collecting vintage treasures, especially from her local flea markets or *loppis*. The librarian in her enjoys cataloguing her finds according to their age, use, and origin. When it comes to displaying her treasures, she clearly has an amazing eye. She puts the items she loves on her shelves and walls, and stows small or awkwardly shaped items, such as old postcards, ink bottles, pens, and pencils, in her collection of boxes. She always wanted to be a museum curator but instead channels her love of curating into her home gallery. Here she creates wondrous assemblages of recycled objects that combine to take on new meanings. She continually changes and develops her wall displays to keep her ideas fresh. It is this delightful sense of play that I love about Ilse's walls.

Ilse Runow Raihle
Journalist
Location: Ystad, Sweden

← Ilse likes to mix styles and colors to bring out the contrasts between things. Here she combines a 1920s mock bamboo chair, which is typical of Denmark's Art Nouveau or Jugend period, with a 1960s mock rococo armoire. The two very different styles complement each other in a wonderfully jarring way.

↑ Ilse has a brilliant eye for a bargain and picked up this 1960s Palmgren's handbag for next to nothing at a flea market. When not in use, handbags should surely be shown off on your walls!

← This 1950s teacup is by Danish porcelain manufacturer Bing and Grøndahl. The turquoise teacup, shoes, and orange teapot (seen on the opposite page) form a beautiful trio.

→→These shoes
are from a 1950s
children's shoe
store that was
closing down. Here
they are displayed
on top of the mock
rococo armoire.

This 1950s
miniature Japanese
teapot is part
of a complete
miniature teaset.
It is made from
delicate
porcelain, hand-
painted with
intricate design
details.

Non-Functional Functionalism

Ilse has a collection of children's shoes—
some are stored away in boxes, others,
like these, she has on show. She uses
them as decorative pieces on tables and
shelves. "Many people would say putting
shoes on a table brings bad luck," she
explains, but she does not believe in such
superstition. Ilse is also fascinated by
Japanese design and loves the tiny scale
of Japanese porcelain teasets. As Ilse has
proved, when functional objects are
taken out of context, they can inspire
a new curiosity.

Traveling Without Moving

Ilse loves to collect vacation souvenirs and vintage travel items at her local flea markets. It makes her feel as if she has actually been to those destinations. She loves objects that "tickle the imagination" and take you places. The world conjures up such diverse aesthetics—it's wonderful to see them collected and mixed on a wall.

Ilse found this vintage suitcase market. It still has hotel stickers on it that speak of tales and adventures from a time long gone.

↑These German dolls' heads are striking, especially the way Ilse has displayed them in a black-velvet-lined box with a gold picture frame. This bold new context gives them a stage to perform on. Ilse loves objects that have strength and are not over-cute. These dolls fit the bill perfectly and have become an intriguing art piece.

←This lady is an example of 1920s Swedish embroidery. Ilse is drawn to its simple, romantic style and enjoys the way it sits on the wall among the other small picture frames and masks.

➔ The higgledy-piggledy nature of the frames and objects on the wall is beautiful. Everything has, in fact, been perfectly considered, but it is the underlying spontaneity that turns the display into something with heart and style. I love the way Ilse boldly uses her intuition. Your gut instinct is always right when it comes to display.

Ilse's open shelves in all their glory. She has a passion for boxes and tins of all shapes and sizes, and fills them with some of her treasures, such as artificial flowers, children's shoes, old ink bottles, and other finds.

Ilse collects jigsaw puzzles and enjoys working on them for a few hours each day while listening to audio books.

Boxes of Happiness

Ilse loves storing small treasures away in beautiful boxes and tins as well as putting them out on display. Her collection of colorful patterned and textured storage boxes is worthy of display in its own right. She piles them one on top of the other on her shelves so they create a beautiful patchwork-quilt effect. Her box collection hails from all parts of the world. Ilse says she has a pretty good sense of what is stored in each box, but it doesn't bother her if she doesn't know exactly. Part of the fun lies in opening a box and finding a lovely surprise inside.

↑Some of the vintage items in Ilse's collection are simply too big or too awkwardly shaped to fit in a box. Items ranging from the bizarre to the banal are jam-packed on this shelf, where they create a thought-provoking visual feast.

➜➜A Japanese box mingles with an old Dutch chocolate box, a vintage leather-covered box, and a lustrous snakeskin box. One box even contains an array of smaller and smaller boxes, like a Russian Babushka doll.

I love the organized, eclectic chaos of Ilse's stacked boxes.

SPLENDID SPLENDOR

The dining room decor has remained the same since the house was built in the 1940s. The heavy table and ornate chairs and sideboard are typical of that time. This room is for socializing, so Ilse feels she doesn't want to bring too much of her own personality into it. She loves the room because it is full of light and has a great view over the garden.

→Ilse is unstoppable when it comes to collecting shells. She loves their other-worldly beauty. "The shapes, colors, everything about them is fascinating," she explains. "The seas are so polluted nowadays that fewer and fewer seashells are being formed. I act as a 'shell rescuer' and have a collection in most rooms."

↓Ilse has dozens of teasets and dinner services. This teaset was used in the Swedish TV series *Wallander*, which was filmed in Ystad. Ilse picked it up at a local sale when the filming was over. Ilse loves its combination of bright blue and gold. She thinks it looks rather magnificent and Russian. She uses different dinner services to complement different meals.

Baroque Bohemian

Ilse says she is a "Baroque Bohemian." "Baroque" is her way of explaining how she exaggerates and does things to the extreme—like collecting a mass of things that she doesn't really need. "Bohemian" describes her laid-back approach to her home. In short, she's not interested in tidying things away. As she says, "I can appreciate the typical clean IKEA style that other people have in their homes, but I couldn't live somewhere that reminds me of a dentist's waiting room. I'm more of a Baroque-Bohemian person. I enjoy clutter and color."

← This earth-toned
display wall mixes
the tribal with
the kitsch and the
unnerving with the
naive to wondrous
effect. Ilse
bought the tribal
masks (top row)
in Uganda when she
was working there
for the Swedish
Red Cross. She
loves the mystique
that surrounds
such masks and the
fact that, when
she walks into the
room, they appear
to be looking
straight at her.
Ilse's collection
of small bottles
stands in a
typographer's case
(far left). She
found the wicker
display case (near
right) at a flea
market. It's
perfect for her
collection of
1950s and 1960s
souvenirs made
from shells. The
empty frame
(bottom left) also
comes from a flea
market. Ilse
thinks it's late
twentieth century.
She's still
looking for the
perfect picture
to put in it.

SARAH SAYS

The walls are a constantly evolving conversation between housemates past and present.

Studio Life/
Life Studio

Established in 2007, Theatre de la Mode (T d l M) is an
international menswear brand. Creative Director Christopher
Kelly's classic cuts mix perfectly with modern fabrics and it
seems as if this business idea of blending the diverse is what
inspires his home/studio.

Christopher lives in a warehouse space in Hackney in East
London. He shares it with Louise O'Hare, who is a curator,
Jenny Patterson, a photographer, and Jonathan Bryan-Franks,
a silver dealer. Jonathan is also Christopher's business partner
and owns the property.

There is a sense of constant change in this live/work space, of
ideas being churned over, and of nothing being too defined.
Prop designers for T d l M shows are at work on various large-
scale projects using a variety of materials, pattern-cutters are
cutting away, and Jenny is cooking up something delicious in
the kitchen. There's clearly a sharing of skills going on that
encourages creativity and is lovely to watch.

Christopher Kelly
Creative Director
Theatre de la Mode
Location: London

↑This embroidered picture was made by
Christopher's friend Vanessa de Silva who,
until recently, lived in the warehouse.
I love the idea that the essence of a
person lives on in their possessions, and
especially in things they've made.

←←The unique space captures something of
each of its inhabitants, past and present.
Louise's Damien Hirst skull sketch, which
she was given when working with Hirst on
a show, sits perfectly with the embroidered
face, with Jenny's 1980s Liberty sofa that
came from her parents' home, and with
Christopher's junk-store treasures. There's
a delicate beauty in the transience of
all the people who have left their mark on
this space.

These three bird pictures were found at
an antiques market just outside London.
They work really well as a triptych; it
feels as if the birds are chirping to
each other.

A Playful Soul

As soon as you enter Christopher's home, not only do you feel the creativity at work, but you also sense the place's playful soul. It's everywhere in the choice of furnishings and accessories, but nowhere is it more evident than in the way playfulness has actually become part of the various displays.

The people who live here are all obviously having fun together, which feels joyful and free.

Jonathan bought the mirror from a bric-a-brac store. He likes the way it works with the Barbie dolls attached to it. The Barbies came into his life one night when a friend stuck them to Jonathan's head!

↑The rabbit sits happily on top of an incredible 1890s cabinet that mimics a shelf full of leather-bound books. The cabinet has been in Jonathan's family for years.

→The ceramic rabbit was a much-loved birthday gift from Jenny to Christopher.

CERAMIC
PETS—PERFECT
FOR URBAN
LIVING

→The ornately patterned, warm-colored upholstery fabrics, cushion covers, and throws create little dens of coziness in the concrete and wooden floorboarded ware-house. It's clear that the room hasn't been "made over" in one fell swoop but is slowly evolving. I love the sensitivity of this approach.

The green cupboard in the living area is actually the top section of the kitchen dresser. This is recycling with love and it really works.

"Walls" of lush greenery help to divide this large warehouse space.

Christopher collects all sorts of hats and was especially pleased to find this fencing mask in the street outside his house. Street finds are the best.

Christopher happened to find this playing card. He thought that gave it a mystical quality and that the card must surely have some special meaning.

"Shad" the dog (the name "Shad" appears at the bottom of the picture) features on Christopher's bedroom wall. He bought the picture from a thrift store in the south of England and can't be sure if Shad is the name of the dog or of the artist. He likes to think it's the dog's name and has decided that if he ever gets a dog, he'll call it Shad.

←←The "pattern wall" was Christopher's idea for storing the mountains of T d l M patterns that have accumulated over the past four years. Each pattern is clearly marked and classified according to season and garment style. Christopher uses the same method of categorization for his patterns as he does for his collections of ephemera. That way there's no divide between work and play.

SARAH SAYS

Open kitchens are welcoming and the warmth of this one seeps into the whole studio space.

Show-Off Collections

Collecting is such a beautiful way of exploring an idea. As you collect, you devise a classification system that you know and understand. Sometimes you keep your collections filed away secretively in a book or box, but when you show them off and display them, then you open yourself up to people's questions. This form of self-expression can be so exciting.

➜Why have one lamp when you can have twelve? More is definitely more when it comes to collecting. All these lamps together create an enormous, layered, and totally unique chandelier.

Each lamp tells a story so a number of stories must be hanging from this ceiling. They somehow bring more life into the room. Christopher recalls how the Chinese lanterns came from a New Moon party. He and his friends ate a Chinese takeout meal beneath the lanterns while Jonathan read ancient Chinese stories about the New Moon. They ended the night by eating Chinese mooncakes in the moonlight on the roof of the warehouse.

中秋佳話

SARAH SAYS
A room full of stories brings out the imagination in people. No wonder they have such great parties here!

CONVERSATION PIECES

Litter your home with things likely to provoke questions. Showing who you are is so much more fun than telling people who you are!

The Incredible Hulk walkie-talkie is one of a pair that Christopher shared with a friend. They lived in a four-storey house and used the walkie-talkies to communicate between floors. When they left the house, each kept his Hulk.

When Christopher moved to London in 2000 he began a collection of teacups, plates, and teapots. His aim was to build a full teaset using orphaned pieces. He has well exceeded that now but just can't stop collecting.

Chapter 2

Twists Of Modernity

A Modernist Smile

Wayne Hemingway is an iconic British designer who has turned his hand to everything from high-street fashion to designing radios to huge housing projects. He is also the driving force behind a major new vintage fashion, art, and design festival.

Wayne and his wife Gerardine live in a stunning mid-century-modern-style home that was designed by Gerardine herself. When building the house, the Hemingways stuck strictly to a budget, using inexpensive industrial materials such as breeze block (cinder block) and metal girders, buying their kitchen units from IKEA, and working in a good dose of recycled and vintage items. Their creativity is apparent everywhere you look, alongside their sense of fun and playfulness.

↑The Hemingways bought this vintage Chinese fan in a rummage sale in Sussex. It's interesting to find objects from far-flung countries in your local sales. It feels as if they have had a story before they have even met you, and then their story starts to merge with yours.

→The lightbulb lamp comes from a flea market, the bowl was bought on a ski vacation in Norway, and the cushion fabric is recycled from the linings of Red or Dead clothing. The mural uses the Hemingways' own print, based on an iconic Tretchikoff painting, and is available from Surface View. The setting makes a grand statement that reflects the originality of the owners.

This wooden cabinet was bought in Melbourne for £30. Shipping it over to England added somewhat to the price but it was most definitely still a bargain. The unusual Art Nouveau-inspired carving makes it a real statement piece.

Wayne Hemingway
Designer, Co-founder of Red or Dead, Chairman of the South Coast Design Forum, Chair of Building For Life
Location: Sussex, England

VALUABLE INVALUABLES
The Hemingways have created loving interiors where flea-market finds sit comfortably alongside recycled fabrics, and furniture they have designed themselves.

↓Light streams through this invigorating open-plan cooking/living space. Its design is minimal yet also fun and unique. The irregular door frames, for example to the storage cupboard perched high on the wall, add to the quirky appeal. It's a modern house with loads of personality.

➔➔This eggstand brings a smile to everyone's face when they realize that the eggs are actually the tonsured heads of the monks.

A Touch of Rebellion

Red or Dead, the fashion company founded by Wayne and Gerardine Hemingway in 1982, was all about turning fashion preconceptions on their head and making the uncool cool. For example, Red or Dead sold Dr Martens, the previously ignored workwear shoes; as a result the brand became one of Britain's fashion phenomena of the 1980s. Wayne and Gerardine's rebellious streak hasn't dulled over the years. They use stone cladding and pebbledash, both usually considered architectural no-no's, on the exterior of their lovely family home in Sussex, and they have turned house design literally on its head, by putting the bedrooms downstairs and this large open-plan cooking/living space upstairs so it benefits from the light.

Interior Reincarnation

The Hemingway home is full of recycled materials, utilized in an inventive and modern way. Their fantastic boat sofas have had many lives. Initially found abandoned by the sea, the boat from which they were made was restored and became the family's prized boat. A friend then borrowed it and it was later shipwrecked and broke into many pieces. Wayne and Gerardine managed to salvage and recycle every bit, using some to make this pair of comfortable sofas. Other parts were used to make the garden shed, and the rest became the tree house in the garden (see page 62). Wayne described the whole process like being a chef and using all of an animal's entrails in his cooking: "Every bit of that boat went to good use... I like to think of it as upcycling to infinity!" It's great to see items living on in other formats. It certainly feels as if this boat is much happier in its new sofa incarnation.

Even the sofa cushions have been recycled. They are made from leftover Red or Dead coat linings.

↑The curved sides of the boat are beautiful and bold and the sofas are amazingly comfortable. Comfort is ultimately the number one requirement for a sofa.

→Wayne received the oversized "notepad table" at the end of one of the sofas as a gift from a student. It works really well as both a coffee table and a notepad. The oversized lamp is Italian but bought in Amsterdam. I really enjoy the way the Hemingways have played with scale in this room. Anything really small, such as a pencil or a notepad, that has been made big always makes me smile.

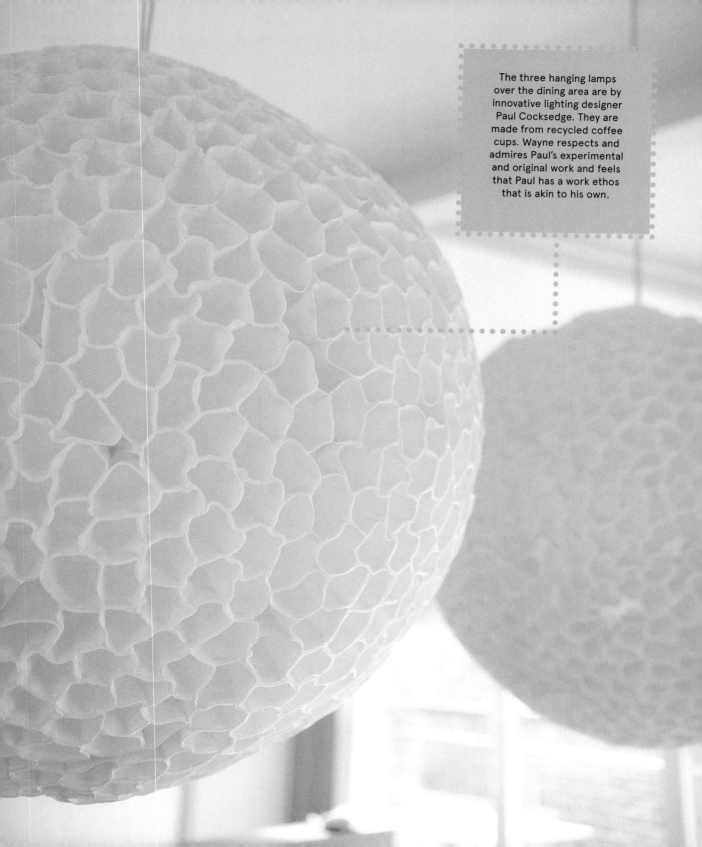

The three hanging lamps over the dining area are by innovative lighting designer Paul Cocksedge. They are made from recycled coffee cups. Wayne respects and admires Paul's experimental and original work and feels that Paul has a work ethos that is akin to his own.

Wayne enjoys this vintage dartboard and displays it as if it were an art piece. The same is true of the periodic table below. I love vintage board games. They often have brilliant graphic shapes and are wonderful pieces to show off on your walls.

↑Wayne was asked to design a radio for teenagers and the result was the Bug Radio standing on the sideboard above. It is based on the film character ET. Stylish bags from IKEA stand beneath. The Hemingways have always believed that good design can also be affordable.

➔The simple lines and pale yellow color of this 1950s dresser make it so beautiful. The metal handles add a functional appeal, while the knitted dogs and donkey figurine on top soften the whole display with a humorous touch.

The dogs on the dresser are sherry-bottle covers knitted by Wayne's grandmother.

Passion Perfect

Dreams and passions need to be nurtured and it's clear from the way in which Wayne categorizes and displays his collection of 7,000 records that he cherishes his love of vinyl. Wayne has developed a unique classification system based on differently colored and shaped stickers: white dots indicate classical music, green dots are for dance and boogie, blue dots are for modern soul, yellow rectangles are for boogaloo, blue rectangles are for disco, green triangles are for punk and new wave, and gold stars are for northern soul. And if that weren't enough, each group is arranged alphabetically.

←The graphic shapes on the wallpaper echo the lines of the modular shelving. Gerardine has designed the innovative modular shelving to hold Wayne's record collection and speakers.

Curating your collections in a methodical way means you have to think about each item, digest what it means to you, and devise a system that reflects the way you feel.

←These remarkable Harp Chairs (1962) are by Danish designer Jørgen Hovelskov. They are like sculptures in their own right yet are wonderfully comfortable to sit on. Their striking shape is based on the bow of a Viking ship. It underlines the musical essence of this part of the house.

Play More

The Bauhaus philosophy—that play is at the root of all creativity—is part of the DNA of the Hemingway house. There is a climbing wall and a table-tennis table in the open-plan living space alongside Wayne's record collection, and a tree house in the garden (see page 62).

For me, my best ideas always come from "play." This is when you can tap into real passions and ideas ring true. Wayne and Gerardine's sense of play is inspirational!

⬇Elvis Costello is one of Wayne's favorites. Old record sleeves are often beautiful objects in their own right. They are worthy of display and link us with the past.

⬅You don't see many climbing walls in homes but this shows not only how much fun they are, but also that they can be rather beautiful, with all their bright, colorful, odd-shaped nooks. This one was inspired by the children's passion for climbing on a family trip.

⬆The modular display system is Gerardine's bespoke design for Wayne's speakers and records. It is always a struggle to find a home for such items, but I like the fact that the Hemingways celebrate them instead of hiding them.

→The "musical coat rack" on a wall in the garden has become more of a display item than something functional. It adds fun and personality to the garden.

The tree house in the garden is made from recycled pieces of the family boat (see page 54). The garden fun continues with a tennis court, swimming pool, summer house, gym, and chicken coop. The upstairs cooking/living space has an entire wall of windows overlooking the garden, so the garden feels very much part of the house.

There is a sense of cheeky playfulness going on between Wayne and Gerardine. Wayne brought home these squirrel figurines from a garden center and left them in the garden for Gerardine to find. They have remained, which means Gerardine has okayed them. As Wayne says, "They've become our friends."

Found in a rummage sale, the decorative coat rack now takes pride of place on a garden wall, proving that indoor furniture can work outdoors.

Wonder Fuel

Björn Springfeldt has an open heart to life and all its enigmas. His eyes reveal a wealth of wisdom but he is clearly still seeking more. Former head of the acclaimed Museum of Modern Art in Stockholm and of the Museum of Malmö, Björn's personal collection focuses on young, emerging artists. As he says, "With the knowledge that I have of the origins of art and tradition, I feel awe, joy, and eagerness living with works by young artists, who have the power to explore the enigma of life in new ways."

Björn bought his derelict house overlooking the sea 20 years ago, after it had been destroyed by fire. He and his wife have restored it so it now stands proudly, with a beautiful front room and mezzanine forming their amazing home gallery. Björn loves being surrounded by his wonder walls, saying that they fuel his imagination. He likes to curate the pieces in his home as he would the works in a gallery, juxtaposing pieces to bring out their contrasts, rather then presenting them as "a collection." Collections, he feels, say more about the collector than about the items in them, whereas playing on the contrasts between the items allows them to do the talking.

Björn Springfeldt
Curator, Former Director of
the Museum of Modern Art,
Stockholm
Location: Värmdö, Sweden

←The Graphic Plus lamp is by Lars Englund and dates from the mid-1990s, while the masterful painting, *Painted Fields and Sky*, is by Jesper Nyrén. The artist painted the view looking through a prism. I love the painting's breathtaking transitions from dark to light.

↑Björn holds a hand with a pointing finger by Lotta Hannerz, a giant variation of which floats in Stockholm harbor, the finger rocking back and forth menacingly. The giant version is unnerving yet comical. I've always loved the piece so it's great to see its original mini version.

Broken Abstract (2007)is by August Sörenson. It depicts a battered, tear- and blood-spattered face with sticking plasters. It's certainly not one's average idea of a living-room piece, but that is what I like about Björn's interiors. He embraces friction in a room and manages to create beauty from it.

←←**Previous pages**
Ebba Matz made her
dogs entitled
Connecting Worlds,
in 2001 for a show
in Washington DC.
These two were
exhibited there,
together with
dozens of others.
Björn explains:
"The dogs stand
looking curiously
forward but can't
move further than
their leashes
allow. The same
goes for us
perhaps ...?"

→This piece by
Lotta Hannerz is
suitably entitled
Cheese (2004).
You can make out
that it's like
a skull looking
back at you. It is
reminiscent of *The
Scream* by Edvard
Munch. Björn
explains that man
is the only animal
that is aware that
it will die, but
humor helps us
to cope with this
horrifying fact.
"Smile in the face
of death" seems to
be what Hannerz is
proposing here or,
perhaps, simply,
"say cheese," just
as you do when
your photo is
being taken.

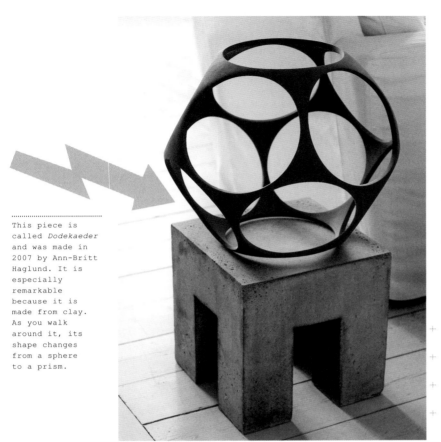

This piece is called *Dodekaeder* and was made in 2007 by Ann-Britt Haglund. It is especially remarkable because it is made from clay. As you walk around it, its shape changes from a sphere to a prism.

Making Sense of Life

Making art is about making sense of life and in this it is akin to storytelling. I love the stories that Björn tells. He does so in a poetic, awe-inspiring, and somewhat hypnotizing way that leads you to think, question, and draw your own conclusions. The same might be said of a work of art. Take, for instance, *Solips*, by Kent Karlsson (1993), pictured on page 48. Here, Karlsson has filled Marja's shoes with concrete. They represent Marja walking through the world and through her life. The candles in the shoes are intended to be lit to mark a celebration or the passing of time, such as a birth or death.

←*Island in Venice* (2004) was made by Ebba Matz when she was invited to the world-famous Berengo glass studio. She asked her master blower to blow a *fiasco*—an unstable round-bottomed bottle. She then had him hit the blowpipe on the floor, making the bottle implode and create a double *fiasco*, which was filled with silver nitrate. This is the beautiful result. It seems that two wrongs can make a right!

SARAH SAYS

Bathroom walls are a great space to have fun with. As you lie in the bathtub you can contemplate your own private gallery.

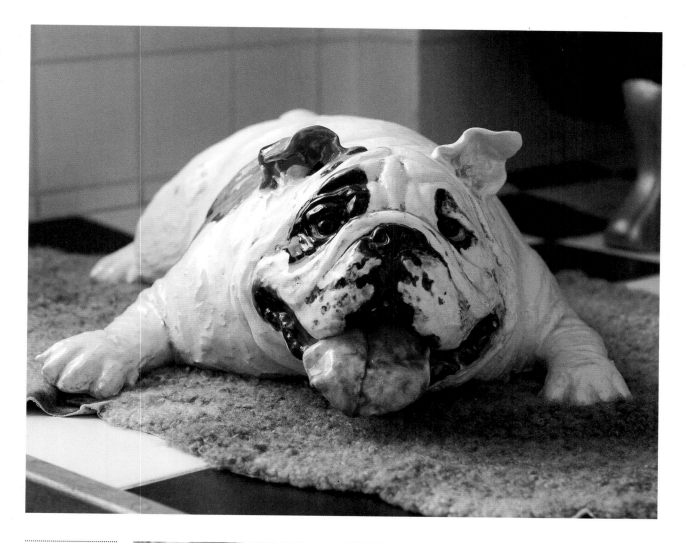

I love this bathroom—it is full of drama and intrigue. Malte the ceramic dog is spreadeagled on the floor; he is so lifelike you can almost hear him panting. A mass of mysterious silicon daisies are scattered around; they are both delightful and melancholy, while the black bathtub is like a giant chess piece on the checkered floor.

These silicon flowers are some of the 40,000 made by hand by Roland Persson in 2000 for an installation entitled *Loves me, Loves me not*. I like the way Björn has sprinkled them around the bathroom like fairy dust.

Malte, the incredibly realistic and humorous glazed ceramic bulldog, was made by Frida Fjellman. When Björn's guests use the bathroom, they joke that they are going to visit Malte.

→→and→This work, *Pain*, was made by
Erik Dietman in 1976 from real bread
that he then glazed. *Pain*, in French,
means "bread" but of course Dietman
intends the work's title to be a play
on the English word "pain." This is
definitely a piece that makes you ask
questions. I love the way Björn has
placed it above the door so it leads
your eye to the fantastic painting on
the wall of the next room. Alongside
the door is a vintage Swedish stove,
one of many in the house. Its beautiful
vintage detail sits perfectly with the
modern art.

A New Way to Communicate

Björn recalls the story in *Gulliver's Travels* by Jonathan Swift. When Gulliver visits the Grand Academy of Lagado in Balnibarbi, he learns of a project for the abolition of all words. Instead, people have to express themselves by showing things that they carry around with them. As Gulliver says, "Therefore the room where company meet who practise this art, is full of all things, ready at hand, requisite to furnish matter for this kind of artificial converse."

In many respects, I find this similar to the way in which people like Björn Springfeldt express themselves through the objects in their homes. Seeing people's personal collections gives you an intimate insight into their true nature, into what really drives and motivates them. It is almost like communicating in a new language.

PAIN

JUST ENOUGH
NONSENSE
MAKES SENSE

Björn bought these fossil-filled stones in Egypt after visiting the famed tombs of the Valley of the Kings. They remind him of the incredible fact that the desert was once a seabed.

Wonder Fascinates

Björn started collecting at the age of ten, when the museum owner in his local village showed him his "cabinet of curiosities." This, like the "wonder cabinets" of old, was filled with the weird and the macabre, such as skulls, stuffed animals, and unidentifiable objects in jars.

Björn now has his own collection, which he uses to open and broaden his mind. "Wonder" for Björn is all about expanding his ideas and propelling them forward. This fills him with awe about the world around him.

I love the stories that everything in this collection evokes. Björn's eyes widen as he tells me their stories one by one.

Collector's Paradise

Mini Maximalism

Hiroyo Suzuki lives with her family in a Tokyo suburb, where she designs, makes, and collects buttons in her home studio. She has thousands of buttons and beads sorted and displayed in cabinets, drawers, cake forms, bottles, jars, and containers. This vast and diverse collection of *saji* (the name of Hiroyo's company, which means "small things" in Japanese) looks magnificent and there is a sense of delicate balance and perfect order everywhere.

Ever since she was a child, Hiroyo has loved collecting small things—sheets of paper, pencils, bottles, stickers, and so forth—so buttons are a natural progression. Hiroyo says that buttons have a "mysterious charm" which she explains by adding, "one button is just a button, but to complete a dress you need lots of buttons."

She loves the modern trend for manga and fantasy but also loves vintage and often uses vintage items in her displays. Her work, which also embraces making pins adorned with her buttons and making leather accessories, such as hairbands, camera straps, and keyrings, is tempered by traditional values: she uses old iron tools to punch and cut the leather.

Hiroyo's studio displays are exquisite. She puts them together instinctively, always with her quiet, elegant touch.

Hiroyo Suzuki
Button designer
Saji
Location: Tokyo, Japan

Vintage Italian beads are stored in tiny jars given to Hiroyo by a friend.

↑Vintage Vietnamese buttons, given to Hiroyo by an art teacher, burst out of a vintage bucket hanging on the wall. The buttons, which Hiroyo has attached to strips of wood, are made from bone, shell, wood, and nuts.

→Hiroyo has laid out her walls instinctively but the effect is that of a structured grid, with boxes and containers creating clean, graphic lines. Her work area provides room for her Washi tape (Japanese masking tape), scissors, and the books she uses for inspiration. I love the way she layers fabrics on the wall to create a background for her display. This whole work environment is conducive to her creativity.

← This cabinet was bought at a vintage store in Tokyo. It was used to store yarn but Hiroyo now fills it with her button collections.

Hiroyo recycles old kitchen cutlery and dish drainers to display her collections. That's what I call supermarket style!

↑ This spade was manufactured in a now-disused factory. Hiroyo has stuck buttons on it and turned it into an art piece. I love the way Hiroyo uses her imagination to reinvent objects.

These oversize wooden buttons are Hiroyo's favorites. I like the play on scale created on the wall by their huge size contrasting with the ever so small.

TENDER BUTTONS

Hiroyo bought these boxes in Kyoto. Their graphic pattern reminds her of the shapes of her buttons.

Delightful Details

Hiroyo's attention to detail is astonishing. She considers every last detail of her displays—the distance between the various elements, the heights and sizes of the different objects, even their colors and tones. And she uses the same attention to detail in her work, making everything intricately by hand. Each button is perfectly punched with her iron puncher, every tiny flower is stitched on lovingly, every leather thong is painstakingly attached.

"It's easier to work with lots of small things than with one big thing," she says as she contemplates her craft. I can see how her delightful interiors echo this very humble thoughtfulness.

←This is one of Hiroyo's hairbands made from buttons. One button is vintage and the other is a leather button that Hiroyo made herself.

Buttons of similar sizes collected together in little glass jars become objects of desire.

→Part of Hiroyo's display wall consists of these colorful buttons collected in individual cake forms. They look good enough to eat.

←Hiroyo's pieces of leather are stored in a very methodical way. Even this storage area, with the fantastic colors of the leathers, is inspirational. She buys the leather in a variety of different markets and punches the buttons out of them.

→Hiroyo is fascinated by color and is drawn to flashes of color like a magpie is drawn to anything shiny.

Hiroyo uses traditional iron punching tools to make her buttons. The larger punches are for cutting the buttons themselves, while the pronged punches are to create the holes. She loves working with craft and precision.

→Hiroyo keeps the pieces of leather that are left over when she punches out her buttons. These cobweblike pieces are beautiful objects in their own right.

Hiroyo's extensive collection of manga fuels her fantasy and inspires her work.

← Hiroyo is a fan of manga and her manga books stand in perfect lines on her bookshelves. On the top shelf are meticulously spaced cans, while small, personal drawings are taped on the wall. Hiroyo also has a penchant for vintage SLR cameras, which she collects. She often makes leather camera straps, like those hanging from the pole over the vintage suitcase. This suitcase accompanies Hiroyo when she goes to fairs and exhibitions.

These decorative pins are arranged to perfection on the inside of the lid of Hiroyo's suitcase. She has stitched them with wool in beautiful colors. The finishing touch is the handmade leather button.

As well as hats, Nanae makes hairbands using ribbon, vintage lace, and embroidery, which she finds in various flea markets. She found the material for this hairband in a flea market in Guatemala. She loves its vivid color.

Tales of Travels

Various department stores and boutiques in Japan stock Nanae Matsunobu's fabulous hats and she also hosts several exhibitions a year in order to promote them.

Nanae means "seven" in Japanese, so it's not surprising that Nanae loves collecting objects with the number seven on them. She also loves the color blue, hence the brand name, Sept Bleus (*sept* is "seven" in French), under which she has been selling her hat creations since 1997.

Nanae lives in a charming studio home in central Tokyo where her work is inspired by her travels (especially travels in France, where she lived for a year) and by things she finds when she trawls antiques markets in far-flung places. She is always on the hunt for beautiful, inspirational fabrics and loves combining items from her travels in her interior decorations.

←Nanae's working wall is where she stores and displays her hats and materials, as well as the tools of her trade, such as her hat blocks and sewing machine. On the right, vintage French lace covers some open shelves, calming the effect of the clutter that lies behind. The decorative ladder holds her hairbands.

→Nanae made these dolls as display pieces for a trade show. They were made from the same materials as the hats that she showed. Nanae's friends say the dolls look like her.

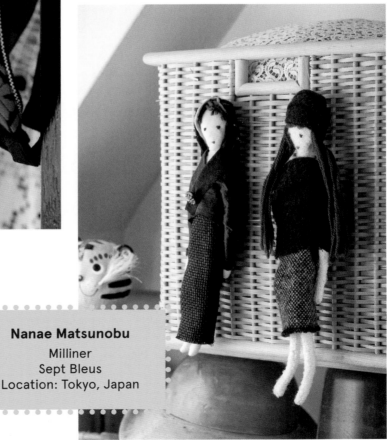

Nanae Matsunobu
Milliner
Sept Bleus
Location: Tokyo, Japan

← Nanae bought these wooden mannequin heads in a flea market in Paris. They are modeling two of her "classic, elegant" hats.

This room is cleverly divided into different areas by a vintage screen and a storage unit. The cushion on the chair comes from Marrakesh and the unusual vase on the table is French. Nanae loves the green color of this compact good-looking Swiss bicycle.

This antique Japanese screen, or *ranma*, fences off the kitchen area. Its graphic pattern is wonderfully simple and modern.

Divide and Conquer

A tall bookshelf and the other unit at right angles to it divide Nanae's studio from the entrance and the kitchen area. They are functional as well as decorative since not only do they work as dividers, but they also house books and a mass of filing boxes. Nanae has placed her favorite objects and personal mementos in front of the books and boxes. The support of her family and friends is important to her, so she likes to display gifts and ornaments which they have given her, to remind her of them and to feel their presence in the room.

Nanae bought these wooden trees in a children's store in Tokyo. They are handmade so each one is slightly different, which Nanae enjoys.

←The jumbled color of the books on the tall bookshelf give it life, while the collection of objects, such as the trees and lighthouses on top, add intrigue.

↑Nanae found the lighthouses in a flea market in Paris and used them in one of her exhibitions. She painted the large one white and uses it to display hats for photoshoots. She loves the shape of lighthouses and can't resist collecting them.

Functional Antiques

Nanae particularly enjoys collecting antiques that she can actually use rather than having them simply as decoration. She loves the way her finds look but is doubly happy when they are practical. This is what I love about vintage finds, too. They are not only one-of-a-kind treasures, but become extra-special when you use them as you know they can never be replaced.

Some of Nanae's favorite finds have been kitchen utensils, vintage containers (see below), and old brass weights (see left).

PUTTING VINTAGE TO WORK

↑Nanae uses these antique weights to hold down her fabrics when she is cutting them out. They are part of her haul from a Parisian flea market.

→Also from a Parisian flea market, these old metal kitchen canisters look very pleasing lined up on Nanae's kitchen windowsill. She uses them to store coffee, tea, spices, and sugar.

When living in France, Nanae came across a snail which she thought was "so peaceful and cute." She immediately began to associate the slowness of the snail with the slower (compared to Tokyo) pace of French life. She really appreciates the French love of good-quality, painstakingly handmade goods, and refuses to have any of her work made in China. Ever since her find, Nanae has been collecting snails and uses these quirky snail pins in her hat designs.

Chapter 4

Inside Out

Creative Shrines

Ayumi Yamamoto is an accessories designer and has been working from her home studio for seven years. Entering Ayumi's studio is to become engulfed in her wonderful botanical underworld. Dried flowers and leaves hang from the low ceilings, and shrubs and large plants envelop the space. The walls are plastered with layer upon layer of inspirational material that appears to unravel before your very eyes.

Here, on a street famous for its cherry blossom, there is a sense of quiet and calm. Ayumi loves cooking for friends, making all sorts of fantastic purées that she stores in jars. Her humble hospitality make this space so endearing.

→→ Ayumi's studio wall, which inspires her creations, has a wonderful tactile quality. Every time you look at its mass collage, something new reveals itself.

Ayumi Yamamoto
Accessories designer
Murder Pollen
Location: Tokyo, Japan

A toy hedgehog made from rubber and a dried lobster hang from an iron chandelier decorated with dried flowers. The hedgehog is from Bonpoint, a French children's boutique with a branch in Tokyo. Ayumi likes its contradictory softness.

↑Ayumi believes in craftsmanship and uses traditional handworking methods to make her jewelry. She cuts semiprecious stones to mimic plant seeds and she also dyes, cuts, and curls leather to mimic the petals of magnolias and dahlias. Despite its fast pace, Tokyo is also a city of strong traditional values; these strike a chord with Ayumi.

The African doll is named Malan and was a birthday gift from friends. It is made of leather and comes from Klasika, one of Ayumi's favorite Tokyo stores.

←Layer upon layer of items clothe Ayumi's inspiration wall. They include her favorite postcards from friends and items she has picked up on her travels. Ideas gradually emerge from her mass of collected material.

The dried bamboo comes from a shrine Ayumi visited at New Year. She explains that every New Year there is a festival of Divine Work and the Shinto priest hands out some sacred bamboo. This particular grass signifies prosperity in business. The little hanging bag is decorated with an image of Ebisu, the God of Luck. Ayumi chose the bag herself at the shrine. I love the idea of choosing something with a specific meaning to take home with you.

SARAH SAYS
Ayumi's interiors have a spiritual resonance that is true and honest, and so typically Japanese.

Nurtured Nature

There are many natural elements in Ayumi's studio and nature is enormously influential, both on her work and on her spiritual wellbeing. In her hands, plant motifs take on a beautiful symbolism and it is these small references to nature that Ayumi enjoys especially. The simplicity of nature coupled with positive growth comprise for her a secular religion and it is this that nurtures her creativity.

Dried flowers and plants hang everywhere, particularly around lights, which creates a wonderfully dramatic effect. Ayumi made these dried dahlias for an exhibition.

←Here Ayumi displays her treasures and inspirational tidbits on a metal shelving unit. Vintage finds and toys of varying dimensions form mini still lifes on each shelf. The shelving unit's functional, strong, somewhat militaristic quality contrasts with Ayumi's delicate and endearing animal ornaments in a wonderfully intriguing way.

↑This object is a piece of paper art made by Tetsuya Nagata, an artist whom Ayumi respects and admires. He uses traditional Japanese sweet molds and a classic type of Japanese heavyweight paper which has a beautiful tactile quality. The delicate forms he has made for this work are winter vegetables to symbolize growth. I find this piece has such a humble beauty.

← Ayumi made this little feather bird as a toy for her cat, Beniko. The colors are beautifully vivid. Ayumi loves animals and all things *kawaii!*

↓ These skeletons were made by Chichitohtoh, a friend of Ayumi's. The skeletons are supposed to be sisters. Ayumi loves the fact that the hearts are sewn onto their bodies.

Kawaii! (it must be written with an exclamation point) is usually translated as "cute" or "pretty." The word stems from two Chinese characters meaning "can love." For me, *kawaii!* is all about a loving charm, which Ayumi puts at the very center of her creations.

← Ayumi has traveled to many parts of Europe and to the USA, picking up fresh ideas along the way. She loves Western vintage and somehow manages to blend her sense of *kawaii!* with her spiritual side. The result is a beautiful style all of its own that is unique to Ayumi.

↑ This "sock monkey" comes from the USA and is made from old socks. Ayumi has named him Neva. She thinks he is fun and *kawaii!*

↓These vintage
arms come from a
French flea market.
I love the way
Ayumi has framed
them. It adds a
morbid beauty to
these hanging
limbs.

↓↓Ayumi made
these leather
flowers for an
exhibition in
Milan. She handcuts
the leather then
dyes it herself.

ROSE-TINTED VINTAGE

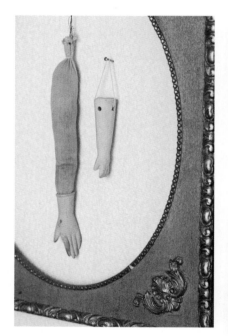

This vintage birdcage has a kingfisher
inside, but the kingfisher is actually a
brooch made by Rusty Thought, designers
with whom Ayumi is friends. Ayumi
respects the work of these designers as
they use traditional Japanese *cloisonné*
and ironworking techniques to make their
beautiful, eccentric jewelry.

This traditional handcarved wooden sweet mold comes from a local flea market. Such molds are beautiful objects in their own right.

Seeds of Joy

Ai is a jewelry designer who lives with her husband and daughter in a studio home on the outskirts of Tokyo. *Ai* is Japanese for "love" and *Titti,* which is her nickname, means "bird." *Titti World* is the name of her company. Ai explains that her creativity and view on the world stem very much from her names. As she says:

"My view of the world is delicate and warm. The name *Titti* reflects the image of a bird. It is the name I feel drawn to and that I want to use as a springboard for my creations. I like the sense of a bird flying so freely that it almost becomes part of the sky."

It is with this in mind that she creates beautifully intricate jewelry and other objects using seeds that she varnishes and threads together. She also incorporates vintage finds, picked up at flea markets, dyeing the antique clothes and lace to suit her purpose. Ai is inspired by artists like Joseph Cornell, who used found materials to create his assemblages. Other inspiration comes from characters in manga cartoons and fairytales, which she reads to her daughter Sakura. Ai has turned her studio home into a place full of nature and love.

↑Ai uses boxes like these, which are stackable, to categorize all her different types of varnished seeds. Laid out in their little compartments, they are like Pick and Mix sweets.

←Ai's world is pure and romantic, and exudes joy. The hanging mandolin and dried-flower bird sing a song of dreams. When the sun streams through the window, the room becomes sepia-toned, almost like a vintage photograph from a bygone age.

Ai Aoki/Titti
Jewelry designer
Titti World
Location: Tokyo, Japan

←Ai draws inspiration from nature and loves the shapes created by seedheads like these. She has stuck them to the wall using tape and has captured their beauty in a frame (see picture opposite).

This is an embroidery of a girl's face that Ai is working on to make part of a bag.

➜This proud and beautiful bird, or *Titti*, of which this is a detail, is constructed from dried plants and flowers. It was made for an exhibition by a friend. Ai loves the way birds fly freely through the sky. She likes to capture that sense of gliding, joy, and free spirit, and tries to imbue her creations with it.

←Ai treats one wall of her studio as though it were a sketchbook, sticking ideas in progress on it and mixing sketches on paper with pieces of textile.

Captured Moments

By carefully drying and varnishing her plant material, Ai manages to capture their delicate beauty forever. There is so much poetry and sensitivity in the pieces that she creates, and their simple meanings and references are so honest that they never appear saccharine or twee.

Ai delicately
threads her
handmade seed beads
to make a necklace.

←This is Ai's workspace, where she fashions her various found objects. Her work has more than just visual impact; it also communicates through its tactile nature, through the smell of the dried plants, and through the sound they create, such as the noise made by the dried grasses rubbing together.

→These child's shoes belonged to Ai's daughter, Sakura, but Sakura has long since grown out of them. Ai has filled them with dried flowers and they now provide a lovely memento of Sakura's childhood.

←This huge painting of a tree is one that Ai made with her daughter, Sakura. Working together, they have collaged to the tree images of insects, birds, and popular cartoon characters, which Sakura loves. One of her favorite characters is the old man Kobito, whose picture in the painting children have to try and spot.

↓This detail of the tree painting shows a heron with a butterfly in its mouth. Ai says she is very much inspired by the French artist Nathalie Lete, who creates collages using a variety of found media.

Sakura created this colorful object as a small stool to sit on. She says it is a unicorn. I love its vivid pinks and yellows.

→Vintage postcards that Ai bought on vacation in London are lovingly displayed on the wall. The lamp is from ATP, her favorite local Japanese vintage store, which has a fantastic collection of vintage from all around the world.

← In this corner of her studio home, dried plants and flowers hang from a long piece of driftwood that Ai found on a trip to the seaside.

These flowers, berries, and seedheads have first been dried, then varnished, then left to dry with clothespins to hold them in place. The display is a visual feast.

Childhood Dreams

There is an innocence to Ai's work and her displays that is natural and open. She has a childlike fascination with manga and with Victorian botanical drawings. Sakura often plays while Ai works and it is beautiful to note that, through Sakura's eyes, Ai sees the world with even greater wonder and awe.

Shapes and Forms of Beauty

Åsa Stenerhag is a designer for the leading Scandinavian fashion brand Filippa K, which is synonymous for its simplicity and quality. Her home is calm, simple, and creative. She has made it a place where she can relax and feel at one with herself—her very own temple. You sense her curiosity and openness to the world emanating from this space, which makes it feel poetic, yet also ordered and balanced. Åsa is clearly searching for beauty, but the harmony and flow of her thoughts means that there is a slow ease to the manner in which she does so. Nothing is forced and unnatural. She experiments with shapes and forms in small, touching ways and with a tenderness toward her materials. There are not too many things in her home but "just enough"— *lagom* in Swedish, one of my favorite Swedish words.

↑Åsa loves using Japanese papers and is fascinated by the way thin papers are affected by inks and water. She thinks the folds and wrinkles that result are part of the beauty of the finished piece.

→These are all works that Åsa is experimenting with. She has taped them to the wall using masking tape so she can study them more carefully. Åsa is constantly working toward finding the perfect balance between design, material, and form, drawing inspiration for her fashion designs from nature.

Åsa Stenerhag
Fashion designer
Location: Stockholm, Sweden

↑Åsa has been making what she calls her "Antiques Papers" from a young age. She soaks different papers with ink, then crumples them, unfolds them, and leaves them to dry. The surfaces this process creates are fascinating. These particular works are made using silk paper, which comes as a surprise as they look solid and heavy, as though they were made from clay or plaster. Åsa enjoys this play with form— the fact that a material is not always what it seems.

Here at her desk is where Åsa experiments with shapes and forms, colors and textures. She might start by examining a collection of stones, then will echo their shape, texture, and color in a piece of fabric or in the cut of a garment.

Buddhism resonates with Åsa since the Buddhist ideals of simplicity echo those of Swedish Minimalism.

◀◀**Previous pages** Åsa's home studio is where she experiments with ideas and techniques. Her creativity is completely intuitive; she describes it almost like a seventh sense: "I have to process things inside myself, then, suddenly, I know exactly how to do something, without really understanding how I've reached that point."

Åsa's creativity even extends into the living area. The art she creates in her home informs her commercial work but also stands on its own merits as art. All her displays come from the heart; they have a wonderful truth and honesty about them.

Works in Progress Work

Åsa likes the fact that there is a sense of a "work in progress" to the walls of her living room. She loves to create a variety of still lifes, mixing together objects that harmonize, such as souvenirs from her travels, found natural objects, textiles bought in different corners of the world, and old and new furniture.

A room like this reminds me of gathering a group of friends together for a celebration. They bring their different ideas and thoughts, with you at the center of things, and somehow help you to see yourself more clearly.

LET YOUR DISPLAYS EVOLVE AROUND YOU

←Åsa's studio is a calm white space with white walls and white-painted floorboards. This provides an environment where Åsa's thoughts can flow freely. The items on the wall are Åsa's own artworks, magazine tearsheets, souvenirs, and other tidbits of inspiration.

→These dry leaves in Åsa's studio are a beautiful color and an interesting shape. As they have dried, they have become molded, like a sculpture. Åsa finds it fascinating to look at them up close and see how the veins of the leaves form a distinctive pattern. Perhaps this piece of inspiration might find its way into the design of a garment's sleeve.

SARAH SAYS
When looked at closely, the ordinary can be extraordinary.

Micro Macro

Åsa draws inspiration on a macro level from friends and travel but she also looks at life on a micro level and sees beauty in the detail. Her main focus is on nature. Having spent her childhood summers at her Swedish family home surrounded by beautiful woodland, Åsa is truly in tune with the Swedish summer ethos of living the simple life and becoming at one with the outdoors. Åsa's home is a homage to nature and she draws inspiration from this, both in her art and in her commercial work.

Åsa was very inspired when she went to Tokyo for the first time. She noticed how people put little plant shoots in a variety of small bottles in a very delicate and creative way. She loves to see the beautiful root systems. So now, instead of throwing old bottles away, she uses them as vases. She likes to place a collection of them together on a tray. This tray is actually the lid of a box that Åsa also bought in Tokyo.

←I just love the way Åsa sees beauty even in broken eggshells. She explains that they create intriguing shapes and structures, and their matt white surface looks almost like the finest porcelain.

← The sense of balance and the clean, harmonious lines of the objects on this wall give them space to breathe.

↓ This cabinet is in Swedish Grace style and dates from the 1920s. The craftsmanship is amazing and the design is simple yet sophisticated. Åsa loves the fact that this piece is of such remarkable quality. It has stood the test of time, which is the sign of true sustainability.

Opposites Attract

Åsa mixes classic furniture with modern ornaments, vintage buys with finds from nature, manufactured objects with handcrafted items, with such sensitivity. Setting these contrasts one against the other gently and tenderly brings out the differences. You can see the play of these contrasts in every room of her home. It all works together in this calm but assured manner with such ease.

This dramatic piece is an Ettore Sottsass vase from Italy. Its graphic black-and-white pattern applied to a hand-molded form is a perfect example of the marriage of great design and craftsmanship.

Åsa found these stones on a beach. The shapes fit together to create a sculpture-like piece. Åsa likes to collect things from outdoors and bring them home. They serve not only as a reminder of a trip, but also as an inspiration and a decorative element.

Form and Function in Beauty

When things "fit," it is as if a small piece of magic has been worked. In Åsa's home, stones sit perfectly balanced on top of each other, a pair of car jacks acts as the support for a shelf, used bottles are turned into vases, and books are piled on top of each other in perfect balance and with their colors in harmony. The way these things all work together is beautiful in a small yet genius way.

← Everything is pared back to create calm in the bedroom. Fewer questions, more block color, dreamy simplicity.

→ Åsa bought a pair of jacks at a flea market near her country house for next to nothing. She was drawn to them even though she didn't know exactly what she was going to do with them. On the very same day that she brought them home, she found a thick plank in a dumpster. It was the perfect width and now the jacks and the plank work together as a shelf in the bedroom. Sometimes it seems your furniture is just meant to be!

Celebrations of Color

Fairytale Fancies

"Kazuo Umezu is one of those artistic giants who, along with a select few others, created the foundation upon which Japan's immense manga and anime industry rests," writes Patrick Macias, Editor-in-Chief of *Otaku USA* magazine.

Mention Kazuo Umezu's name in Japan and squeals of delight usually follow. He is certainly one of Japan's favorite celebrities—and "celebrate" is what Kazuo does. His house in Tokyo is like a play house that pays homage to all things celebratory. In fact, with its rooms decorated with tinsel and Christmas trees, it is Christmas every day in the house of Umezu.

↓This wreath was a gift from a guest who attended Kazuo's house-warming party. In addition to featuring Kazuo's trademark red and white, the wreath is emblazoned with the face of his manga character, Macchome-man. The Chinese character '祝' on his forehead means "celebration."

↑Kazuo stumbled upon this collection of red glass at a junk store near his house. He loves primary colors and when he collects things he always has them in mind. The doll is Mika Neichan (The Sister Mika), a character from his work *The Antics of Makoto Chan*. It is one of the dolls sold as part of Kazuo's official merchandise.

←Kazuo's hallway features a lot of red set against white. Red is often associated with anger in Japan but red and white symbolize an auspicious or happy occasion. Kazuo also likes this color combination as it makes the red stand out. Stepping into his hallway is like stepping into *Alice in Wonderland*—the effect is totally unreal.

In this image Kazuo presents himself mockingly as a laughing prince dressed in sixteenth-century European clothes.

Kazuo loves stripes and decorated the outside of his house with red-and-white candy stripes. It stands out like a beacon on this quiet, suburban Tokyo street.

Kazuo's style is greatly inspired by Western fairytales and Gothic fantasy, as well as by Walt Disney, Victoriana, and by Japan's other post-war comic artists. His innovative work is fantastical and bursting with color.

He would like the generally conforming Japanese to be more open to self-expression and individuality, and less concerned with functionalism, rigidity, and social hierarchy. There is no doubt that he uses his art to challenge these Japanese tendencies to the utmost.

←This double staircase is Kazuo's magic entrance, where he surprises his guests. He loves to choose something to wear from his extensive costume collection and then pops out from the middle of the staircase making his magical *Gwashi* sign. I like the way he props framed pictures against the walls, turning the whole area into a super display space.

Kazuo's candy-striped house was greeted with dismay by his neighbors and with delight by his fellow artists.

THERE'S NO PLACE LIKE HOME

Extremely Fantastic

Kazuo makes much of extremes in his books—right and wrong, sacred and profane, clean and dirty, male and female, young and old, living and dead. It is no surprise, therefore, that he carries everything to the extreme when it comes to decorating his home. Here, nothing is halfhearted. He does everything with the utmost force, energy, and thoughtfulness, right down to his choice of colors and themes, and the positioning of his various collections. His house is a fantastic fairytale where stories are played out within its various rooms.

In this room, even the ceiling is green, giving a sense of total encapsulation within the color. The white baseboard and ceiling molding stand out dramatically. A "science-fiction" lamp is set into the floor, while the alcove boasts French-style chairs and a table.

←A collection of stripy slippers greets you as you enter the house. It's almost as if, when you put them on, you are transported into Kazuo's make-believe world.

↑↑A stripy scarf is wrapped around a vintage butterfly-bedecked wall lamp.

↑A stripy cap hangs from the white-painted hat stand.

Kazuo's merchandise is to be found all over the house. These dolls dressed like Japanese schoolchildren have the characteristic oval faces and big round eyes. Their screams seem to express both delight and terror.

Delight and Terror

When Kazuo was growing up, his family lived in a small town deep in the mountains of Nara Prefecture. At bedtime his father would tell Kazuo the delightful yet terrifying local legends that featured snake women, malevolent ghosts, and shape-changing spirits. Since then, Kazuo has marveled at the macabre, the grotesque, and the absurd. His work combines grotesque imagery and doe-eyed girls, and has resulted in a whole new literary genre. It has also earned him the title "Godfather of Japanese Horror Comics."

↑Kazuo is an entertainer above all else. His instantly recognizable *Gwashi* sign (the extended pinky, forefinger, and thumb) and his trademark red-and-white striped wardrobe have made him a national institution.

→Kazuo's official merchandise includes these delightfully terrifying figurines.

⬆This little monkey is part of a Kazuo "still life" (see picture opposite). The precision of its placing is so touching. Nothing in Kazuo's home is left to chance or unconsidered. He is a master stylist.

⬅ Part of the same "still life" (see picture opposite), this is the manga Goddess of Romance. She holds up three fingers signifying that you have three attempts to find love. Many of Kazuo's stories involve intriguing numerical superstitions and symbols.

⬆Many of Kazuo's comics have been turned into feature-length films and a great deal of merchandise adorns his home, including these screaming heads, stacked one on top of the other.

Rejoice and Inspire

Andrew loves the idea that someone can walk into his studio home and can rejoice in and be inspired by the fanciful space. Here he has developed a language of self-expression that is heartfelt and unafraid. It is the complete antithesis of modern minimalism, which Andrew feels can often be bleak, anonymous, and uninspiring.

His work "uplifts the spirit, tantalizes the eye, and brings a smile to the face of all who see it," says Philip Hughes, gallery director at the Ruthin Craft Centre in Wales. Appropriately, *Rejoice* was the title of his 2010 exhibition at the Flowers East Gallery in London's East End. Andrew's type of flamboyance is most definitely something to be celebrated.

←←This brooch decorated with a bee was part of an installation that Andrew made. He works with equal vivacity on pieces of all sizes, from his small items of jewelry to life-size winged horses.

↓Andrew often works with mirrors: he is interested in reflections and in how people see themselves. His mirrored pieces change according to whatever is reflected in them. They come to life and appear to dance before your eyes, adding to Andrew's fascination with disguise and dressing in drag.

MIRROR, MIRROR ON THE WALL

➜➜Andrew's sculpture *Roy* (1998) is astonishingly lifelike. You can really sense the sitter's personality. I like the way Andrew has incorporated the nodding dog, which he received as a gift, into the sculpture.

➜The sculpture with the ruff of pearls is of the British painter Matthew Stradling and is called *Matthew in Pearl*. A behatted Burnel Penhaul as Miss Gale Force Wind makes his appearance just behind. Andrew often works with artists he admires and they sometimes portray each other in their work.

In this piece, the panda represents China and the white figurine reading a book represents Lenin. Andrew explains that the message here is a political one—China is looking over Russia's shoulder.

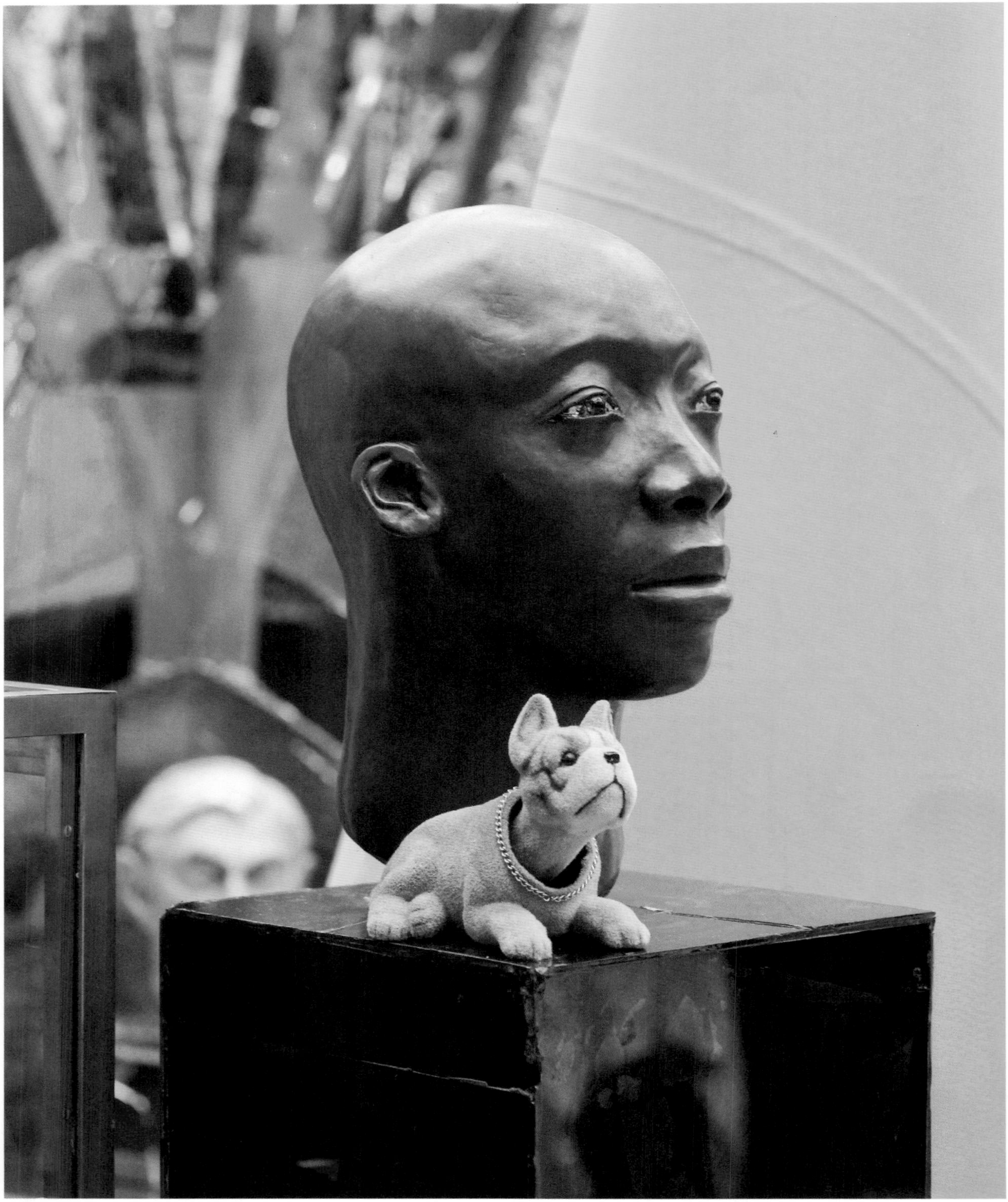

FANTASY VS REALITY

Andrew likes to explore the space between reality and fantasy, using objects, as here, to illustrate ideas and thoughts.

←←←**Previous pages**
This piece, made
from found objects,
is called *The
Mountain* (2001).
It represents a
thirty-year
spiritual journey.

←←Andrew's
stunning *Maria
Callas* (2007)
captures the glamor
of the woman.
Callas was one of
the most renowned
opera singers of
the twentieth
century.

Part of a wall
sculpture entitled
Eventuality
(1997). Made from
mirrors and glass,
this piece
positively glows.

← An interior "window" opens up the space and allows you to see into the fantastic red room beyond. Next to the window is *Irene Worth* (1999). Miss Worth was a star of American and British theater.

Fun and Fancy

I have often wondered why, when we become adults, we are supposed to stop playing children's games, like the party game of Pass the Parcel. Andrew Logan, I think, understands my concern. In 1972 he founded Alternative Miss World. This fantastical beauty pageant—inspired by a visit Andrew made to the Crufts Dog Show—is where thousands join the distinguished judges to see glamorous, mainly male contestants, parade daywear, swimwear, and evening wear. This and much of Andrew's work bears testament to his sense of fun and kitsch.

↑ Andrew's *Taking the Mickey* (2007). I love the extra face attached to the back of Mickey Mouse's head.

The images standing in the foreground and below *Taking the Mickey* are Andrew's sculptures of Sophie Parkin (left), writer, artist, and actor, and her Welsh mother, Molly Parkin (right), painter, novelist, and journalist.

This red iron tealight holder was a present. I love the way Chisa "pops" her reds in just the right places.

←←←**Previous
pages** Ornate
bathtubs should
not be enclosed
in a bathroom, but
should be shown
off. I love Chisa's
proud bathtub
standing on its
plinth; I can
imagine its water
overflowing in a
decadent manner...

←←Chisa bought
this "nest" in
Madagascar. She
uses it to store
her needles, pins,
and threads.

←A three-legged
lamp from IKEA
struts behind the
Madagascan "nest."
Although the lamp
is not big, it
has a handle and
wheels, suggesting,
playfully, that
they are needed
to move the lamp
around.

←An array of boxes are piled on top of each other like an acrobatic display at the circus. They are perfectly askew.

This pair of Vero Twiqo shoes are made from a combination of red enamel, leather, and lace. Chisa's shoe boxes are like old-fashioned wooden shoe-shine boxes. Quality and longevity are important to Chisa, so she always includes care instructions to ensure that the owner will take care of their shoes and keep them forever.

Marvelous Magic

One would expect that if you clicked your fingers, the wall display pictured opposite would spring into life. The boxes would open, the shoes would start to dance, and the horse would begin rocking. It is a scene that seems to have been frozen in time, with cupboards ajar, shoes at a tilt, and the horse almost in motion. This wall display has a beauty that almost sings.

←This rocking-horse light was bought at a gallery in central Tokyo where old furniture is upcycled by the artist Kuromame. Chisa enjoys the idea that new purpose can be given to an old object in this way.

Extravagantly Simple

I love the way Chisa has taken a very simple circular lampshade frame and hanging bulb, and turned them into an ornate chandelier. The bare lightbulb works really well with this almost ridiculous explosion of French linen, toile de Jouy, florals, and upholstery trim. Small beads and bobbles echo the large dangling bead that is the lightbulb.

This chandelier made from vintage fabric and trim forms part of Chisa's Mt. Hari interiors range.

→Here, the intricate detail and hand sewing can be seen up close. Such attention to detail is Chisa's trademark.

The mismatched fabrics and textures of this piece add a sense of homeliness and playfulness to an urban space.

This giant needle is actually one of Chisa's pincushions. I love the absurdity of this piece. Chisa's ideas are quietly bold in this wonderfully charming way.

Scenes To Live With

Chisa stage-manages her space and directs the interiors as if they were scenes in a play. She busies herself, making sure her sets are just right and that her objects/actors are exactly how she wants them. She says that she loves taking things out of context and putting them in newly created worlds. Her playful scenes are thoughtful and truly imaginative.

Chisa designed this folding stool in collaboration with one of the woodworkers she uses for Vero Twiqo. Its beautiful seat is made from woven leather strips. The stool is easy to carry and store.

◄◄Caged shoes hang in this thought-provoking wall arrangement. I love the drama of this display.

→This charming display is full of objects used in unexpected ways, creating a fun juxtaposition of form and function. The scene as a whole arouses your curiosity. Everything is a beautiful surprise.

Chisa bought these tiny shoes as key rings in Paris and has turned them into earrings. I love the idea of wearing your shoes in your ears.

This electric lightbulb bottle is filled with *sake*. Now that's a bright idea!

Index

Acknowledgments

Thank you to all the super designers and collectors who have been my inspiration:

Ilse Runow Raihle

Björn Springfeldt

Åsa Stenerhag

Wayne and Gerardine Hemingway
www.hemingwaydesign.co.uk

Andrew Logan www.andrewlogan.com, his partner Michael Davis, and his trusty assistant Russell Duke
www.riverfragments.org.uk

Christopher Kelly
www.theatredelamode.co.uk

Jonathan Franks
www.ifranks.com

Louise O'Hare
www.publishandbedamned.org

Jennifer Pattison
www.jennifer-pattison.com

Kazuo Umezu
www.umezz.com

Ai Aoki
www.titti-world.com

Nanae Matsunobu
www.septbleus.com

Chisa Nomura
www.verotwiqo.com

Hiroyo Suzuki
www.sa-ji.com

Ayumi Yamamoto
www.murderpollen.jp

Special thanks to the people who made it all possible:

Katrine Hamori (my aunt and vintage mentor)

Akio Fukushima
www.akio-style.com

M. Amano at Shogakukan

Yoko Sato (translator)

Satoshi Hirano (translator)

Coco Tashima
www.paumes.com

Tomo Roberston

Ebony Bizys
www.hellosandwich.blogspot.com

Grace Lee
www.fromasowsear.blogspot.co.uk

Chiho Tsuda
www.chigo.jp

Shoko Ichikawa

Yumi Wakiyama

Christopher Newton

Che Zara Blomfield
www.thecomposingrooms.com

Linda Berlin
www.libraryman.se

Fred Butler
www.fredbutlerstyle.com

Geraldine James at Selfridges

Victor Press at Acne Studio, Stockholm

Graham Rawle
www.grahamrawle.com

Linnea and Adam Springfeldt
www.linneasetdesign.blogspot.co.uk

Bethan Wood
www.woodlondon.co.uk

Laurence Zeegan
www.zeegen.com

Richard Dee (designer and programmer)
www.rich.dee.im

Arthur Guy (programmer)
www.arthurguy.co.uk

Henrik Delehag (Designer)
www.delehag.com

Annette Gray

The team at Squint/Opera, The Doodle Bar, and Poke London

Thanks to the wonderful team at Cico Books:

Cindy Richards, Sally Powell, Gillian Haslam, Hilary Mandleberg, photographer James Gardiner and photography assistant Andrew Swanell, book designer Teo Connor and the No Days Off team.

Thanks to my trusty advisors:

My super sister Alexandra Bagner for helping enormously with the edit

Pushes of literary and design support from:
Jamie Elliot
www.jamieelliott.com

Cecilia Lindren
www.cecilialindgren.com

Christopher Hopkins
www.chris-hopkins.com

Thanks to my Print House studio family: Mardi Latch, Oli and Chloe Jones, Tom Collins, Hannah Gould, Kuba Nowak, Gail Bryson, Aubrey Wade, Sophie Smith, Poly Brannan, Solene Roure, Edward Tull, Richard Mitchell, and Stephen Hignell.

And of course, special thanks for all the support from my family and friends:

Susanne Bagner, Hans Bagner, the Bagner-Jensmar family ,the Bagner-Hicks family—especially baby Celia! The Finlay family, Joanna Peace, Rose Allett, Tara Breeze, Elkie Brown, Alexandra Cunningham, Phoebe D'Arcy Stuart, Lara Bland, Miriam Elia, Lynn Hatzius, Alex Kiehl, Rhiannon McKay-Smith, Beatrice Read, Victoria Saxton, Annie Sturge-Heath, Perican Tahir, Alice Conibere, Jenny Kimmerich, Oliver Wright, and to everyone who has supported Supermarket Sarah.

For more walls go to:
www.supermarketsarah.com